A Matter of Choice

A Twentieth Century Fund Paper

A Matter of Choice

A Critique of Comparable Worth by a Skeptical Feminist

By Jennifer Roback

PP Priority Press Publications/New York/1986

The Twentieth Century Fund is an independent research foundation which undertakes policy studies of economic, political, and social institutions and issues. The Fund was founded in 1919 and endowed by Edward A. Filene.

Foreword

COMPARABLE WORTH IS AN attractive idea. As a matter of fairness and equity, most people will agree that equal pay for equal work or comparable pay for different but comparable jobs makes sense. Yet comparable worth has not won rapid or broad acceptance, probably because it is viewed mainly as a feminist cause. Certainly, the women's movement has been the most ardent advocate of comparable worth, and has worked longest and hardest to make a compelling case on behalf of women in the work force who are either paid less than their male counterparts or who get less in traditional women's jobs than men get in traditional men's jobs. In particular, the campaign for comparable worth has focused on the gap between male and female wages, arguing that its existence is proof, if proof is needed, of continuing discrimination in our society.

As an institution sponsoring and supervising research on public policy issues, the Twentieth Century Fund is not a newcomer in this area. In 1970, in response to the new wave of feminism then sweeping the nation, the Fund assembled a Task Force to examine the status of working women. The Report of the Task Force began with the statement "Men and women in the labor force are not treated equally," then went on to make recommendations for change. Now, fifteen years later, despite some narrowing of the gap between male and female wages, the idea of comparable worth had gained new currency and support. The Fund thought it was time to examine the subject from this new perspective.

In looking for an author of a fresh and cogent analysis of comparable worth, we sought proposals from male and female scholars. The majority either were passionately against or for the idea or took no side at all. Easily the most interesting and provocative of the proposals came from Jennifer Roback, who was then an assistant professor of economics at Yale. She termed herself a skeptical feminist and proposed an approach that gave promise of making a useful contribution to the current debate.

We have not been disappointed. Roback, who is now assistant professor of economics at George Mason University and research associate at the Center for the Study of Public Choice at George Mason, has a clear analytical approach that takes into account supply and demand in the labor market and the peculiar difficulties faced by women who work and also raise a family.

Women now make up a large part of the nation's work force. They can be found in all sectors, holding both the most menial jobs and the most lofty. A good deal of progress has been made in recent years in getting rid of the prejudices and stereotypes about women workers that once prevailed in the market. Needless to say, more must be done. But Roback argues that there are flaws inherent in the idea of comparable worth. Her position may not please spokesmen for the idea. But they ought to pay heed to it.

We think that Roback has done what we expected, which is to stimulate this debate. We are grateful to her for doing so.

M. J. Rossant, DIRECTOR
The Twentieth Century Fund
February 1986

Author's Note

WHEN I REREAD THE PAGE PROOFS for this manuscript on January 31, 1986, three short days after the tragic explosion of the space shuttle, Challenger, I realized that my passing reference to the presence of women in the space program (on page 25) was inappropriate under the circumstances. My first thought was to rededicate this manuscript to the memory of Judith Resnick and Christa McAuliffe, but it seemed presumptuous to dedicate a work which takes a strong position on a highly politicized subject to two such decidedly nonpolitical people. Nevertheless, I think something needs to be said.

All Americans are deeply indebted to McAuliffe and Resnick, but I think that American women owe them a special debt. And the particular kind of debt that we owe them is precisely the kind that policies like comparable worth unfortunately tend to obscure. Christa McAuliffe was a high school social sciences teacher, a job usually considered traditionally female. But she knew the value of her profession and knew that the all too often used phrase "just a school teacher" was nonsense. And so when the opportunity presented itself, she, along with thousands of other teachers, male and female, reached out, and she was chosen. Judith Resnick also reached for something more. She could have been the local piano teacher (she was a classical pianist) or a lab technician, instead she became the second American woman in space.

It is undoubtedly true that many women feel constrained by social and economic pressures to remain in the traditional roles of mother and nurturer, and in the traditional employment patterns that accompanied those roles for so many of our mothers. But it is also true that many women have the courage to challenge those traditions, regardless of society's expectations. Some of these women do unusual things, while others, after careful self-examination, choose to follow the traditional pattern because it suits them, not because it is traditional.

Certainly every thoughtful commentator on women's issues is well aware that women face these choices, and that some women are much more constrained in choosing than others. However, some policies and the advocates who support them tend to focus on the constraints rather than the growing freedom. Comparable worth, for example, is based on the proposition that women are forced into low-paying jobs by social and economic pressure. It focuses on constraints rather than possibilities. It assumes women are afraid rather than courageous; that women are helpless victims, easily swayed by public opinion, rather than autonomous individuals living on their own terms.

The danger of such an emphasis is that is tends to ignore or trivialize the achievements of women. If we truly believe that most women are so constrained that they have no choice but to be secretaries and nurses, then we are forced to see woman astronauts as an anomaly. This is not a far-fetched concern: consider the black civil rights movement as an example. In the last twenty years, a substantial black middle class has developed in the United States, a phenomenon well documented by a prominent black sociologist, William Julius Williams. Yet there is almost no mention of the black middle class in the media or in political debates. White America's image of blacks remains largely an image of a lower class group.

The women's movement is in danger of going the same route. Comparable worth is a major step in a direction that I believe would be tragic for American women in the long run.

This is the debt of American women to Christa McAuliffe and Judith Resnick: no matter what happens in the political arena, the courts, or the media, the example of their courage is not one we will be able to forget.

Contents

To my friend and partner
Rob Morse

*

Many people very generously provided me with source material, among them are Karen Berg, S. Anna Kondratas, Virginia Lamp, Cameron Munter, and Virginia Ross. Deborah Walker provided research assistance.

Preface

I WANT TO MAKE CLEAR at the outset that I consider myself a feminist. I graduated from high school in 1971, just when the women's liberation movement of the late sixties began to attract national attention. I put myself through college by doing a variety of traditionally "male" jobs. I went to graduate school and earned a doctorate in economics, not exactly a field dominated by women. Advancing my career has meant moving several times to different universities, and each time the man in my life moved with me. He followed my career rather than the reverse.

Although I am aware that many of us still feel condemned to tedious jobs by social or economic pressures, I am particularly grateful to live in an era that allows so many women to develop their intellectual and economic potential.

I come from a large, noisy working-class family in the Midwest. Women of my mother's generation seldom pursued full-time careers, but my family supported my aspirations. When I was a graduate student at the university of Rochester, I used to reflect on the story of how Susan B. Anthony (1820-1906), the great champion of women's suffrage, gave her entire savings to the University so it could build women's dormitories and admit women. I liked to imagine her watching me, to make sure I studied hard lest her generosity go unrewarded.

Thus I feel a great personal debt to the women's movement. Thanks largely to its efforts, women's educational and occupational opportunities have expanded to create a whole new variety of social roles.

Yet it is precisely from my dual perspective as a feminist and an economist that I take issue with advocates of the socioeconomic policy known as "comparable worth." Although it has been called the

1

"feminist issue of the eighties," I believe comparable worth will substantially impede the cause of women's economic advancement. If this policy is enacted on a large scale in the public and private sectors, as now appears possible, fewer women will seek traditionally "male" jobs, and those in traditionally "female" occupations will find fewer job opportunities. Nor is comparable worth consistent with the ideological goals of the women's movement; to the contrary, it promises to reinforce many of our most insidious occupational sex stereotypes. Overall, I feel that the women's movement has become obsessively preoccupied with how much money women earn and that this preoccupation is hindering the progress toward women's full emancipation. But before I try to prove these claims, I want to examine what the advocates of comparable worth have in mind.

1. The Legal Background of Comparable Worth

COMPARABLE WORTH, ALSO REFERRED TO as "pay equity," represents the most radical strategy to date for achieving earnings parity between men and women. The term, shorthand for the phrase "comparable pay for jobs of comparable worth," is based on the notion that people who do jobs with comparable worth or value to employers and/or to society are not always paid comparable wages. Pay equity advocates argue two things: that women are systematically segregated into a limited set of "women's jobs" (see Table 1), and that these jobs are systematically undervalued by employers simply because women do them. So even though men and women with the same jobs are entitled to the same pay, women's average earnings are still lower.

Comparable worth first came to national attention in 1977 as a Carter administration policy goal supported by Eleanor Holmes Norton, then chair of the Equal Employment Opportunity Commission (EEOC). By 1980, women's rights organizations were actively espousing the cause; in 1981, comparable worth began to find institutional footing, and since then more than 40 states and 52 municipalities have established pay equity measures.[1]

Now that comparable worth is no longer a theory but a reality, many of its vociferous supporters and detractors have narrowed the terms of their debate to the fine points of policy-making: how best to measure the nature, scope, and extent of wage differentials, and how to make wage adjustments in a fair and fiscally responsible way.

Yet the participants have not yet resolved the central question posed by comparable worth: discrimination. Is the earnings gap between men and women truly a function of discrimination, or might it result from other factors—including choice?

3

Table 1
Some Female Jobs

(Women Workers as a Percent of all
Workers for Selected Occupations, 1982)

Librarians, Archivists & Curators	80.7
Registered Nurses, Dieticians & Therapists	91.8
Health Technologists & Technicians	72.9
Social & Recreation Workers	65.5
Elementary Teachers	82.4
Pre-Kindergarten & Kindergarten	98.5
Sales Clerks, Retail Trade	70.0
Clerical & Kindred Workers	80.7
Receptionists	97.5
Secretaries	99.2
Sewers & Stitchers	95.4
Child Care Workers	96.2
Hairdressers & Cosmetologists	89.5

Source: Statistical Abstract of the U.S., 1984, Table Number: 696, p. 419.

Discrimination

As one of the most explosive terms in the American political vocabulary, discrimination must be carefully defined at the start. The basic definition used by scholars, policymakers, and legislators focusing on the labor force is that discrimination exists when people are paid differently for doing the same work. Excluding a group or groups of people from certain types of work, thus limiting their economic opportunities, may also be described as discrimination. Both meanings have been widely used in the debate over comparable worth.

But both kinds of discrimination are in practice quite difficult to establish. It is hard to tell whether people are really doing exactly the same work and whether they bring identical skills to that work. It is also hard to know if a group of people has been excluded from a given occupation, or whether, because of shared characteristics, they have simply chosen other occupations. If people choose to act in ways that reduce their earnings, there is very little case for intervention. If they are coerced into doing things that reduce their earnings, it is important to know how they are coerced, because different forms of coercion should invite different policy responses.

The push for comparable worth reflects the frustration of the women's movement with earlier legislative efforts to improve women's economic lot. Both the Equal Pay Act (E.P.A.) of 1963 and Title VII of the Civil Rights Act of 1964 were designed to prevent job discrimination of various sorts. Under the Equal Pay Act, employers may not pay employees of one sex less than employees of the other for doing "the same work." (For legal purposes, "the same work" means work of substantially similar content requiring equal skill, effort, and responsibility and performed under similar working conditions. The act allows for four "affirmative defenses" that exempt pay differences based on seniority, merit, quantity or quality of production, or some "factor other than sex.") Thus, equal pay for equal work has been law for over twenty years.

Title VII of the Civil Rights Act protects women and minority workers in more far ranging ways. In addition to guaranteeing equal pay for equal work, Title VII forbids discrimination in initial job assignments and job segregation. Under Title VII, women cannot be denied the opportunity to apply for any jobs, training, transfers, or promotions.[2] Thus, job segregation too has been illegal for over twenty years.

Despite this legislation, and despite rapid growth in the number of women in the labor force, their average earnings continue to lag behind men's. In fact, the ratio of women's average earnings to men's fell from 64 percent in 1955 to 59 percent in 1970, and it remained at roughly that level until 1980.[3] Hence the belief that only stronger, more dramatic government intervention will close the gap.

Comparable worth goes beyond the E.P.A. and Title VII in two important respects. It broadens the definition of discrimination to include wage disparities that do not result either from intentional discrimination or intentional job segregation. And it attempts to equate widely dissimilar jobs according to certain characteristics they may have in common, such as levels of skill, responsibility, and effort. (For example, truck drivers have been paired with secretaries, tree trimmers with nurses.) In doing so, it aims to supplant or at least supplement the market as the primary wage-setting mechanism.

Most champions of comparable worth feel their goal can best be accomplished by adapting a wage-setting technique already firmly entrenched in the public sector (and to a lesser extent in the private sector)—job evaluation.[4] Job evaluation plans, or surveys, have been used within individual industries to set wages for certain jobs since the Second World War.[5] Comparable worth would use job evaluation methods as the basis for ranking all jobs as a means of weeding out discrimination. In its most radical form, this policy would not only operate within individual firms, but also across firms, enforced by the courts and federal agencies. The EEOC and the courts would be required to apply the comparable worth standard, rather than the equal pay for equal work standard, in deciding whether wage discrimination has occurred.

Much of the impetus for pay equity comes from the fact that some employers who use job evaluation surveys do not always pay the same wages for jobs with similar job evaluation scores. For instance, in one of the earliest comparable worth cases, the city of San Jose, California, was charged with paying chemists more than librarians, and carpenters more than legal secretaries—thus, more for "male" jobs—even though these pairs of jobs had similar evaluation scores (see Table 2). Similarly, both Westinghouse and General Electric have paid women's jobs lower wages than men's jobs with comparable job evaluation scores.[6]

Comparable Worth in the Courts

The best known of the early cases involving comparable worth in the public sector is *County of Washington v. Gunther,*[7] decided by the U.S. Supreme Court in 1981. Contrary to popular belief, the *Gunther* case did not endorse comparable worth. The Court decided that the county was guilty of intentional discrimination, in defiance of the Equal Pay Act and Title VII of the Civil Rights Act, because despite similar job ratings female prison guards were paid less than male guards. Thus, in violating its own compensation procedures it had intentionally discriminated. In the Court's words:

> Respondents' claim is not based on the controversial concept of "comparable worth," under which plaintiffs might claim increased compensation on the basis of a comparison of the intrinsic worth or difficulty of their jobs with that of other jobs in the same organization or community. Rather respondents seek to prove, by

Table 2. Sample Comparisons of Job Evaluation Points and Pay

A. Inequality of Pay in Relation to Job Evaluation Points

State	Job Title	Monthly Salary	Difference	No. of Points
Minnesota	Registered Nurse (F)	$1,723	$537	275
	Vocational Education Teacher (M)	2,260		275
San Jose, CA	Senior Legal Secretary (F)	665	$375	226
	Senior Carpenter (M)	1,040		226
	Senior Librarian (F)	898	$221	493
	Senior Chemist (M)	1,119		493
Washington State	Administrative Services Manager A (F)	1,211	$500	506
	Systems Analyst III (M)	1,711		426
	Dental Assistant I (F)	608	$208	120
	Stockroom Attendant II (M)	816		120
	Food Service Worker (F)	637	$332	93
	Truck Driver (M)	969		94

B. Inequality of Job Evaluation Points in Relation to Pay

State	Job Title	Monthly Salary	Point Difference	No. of Points
Minnesota	Health Program Representative (F)	$1,590	82	238
	Steam Boiler Attendant (M)	1,611		156
	Data Processing Coordinator (F)	1,423	65	199
	General Repair Work (M)	1,546		134
San Jose, CA	Librarian I (F)	750	164	228
	Street Sweeper Operator (M)	758		124

Source: Ronnie Steinberg, "Identifying Wage Discrimination and Implementing Pay Equity Adjustments," *Comparable Worth: Issue for the '80s* (Washington, D.C.: U.S. Commission on Civil Rights, 1984), p. 108.

direct evidence, that their wages were depressed because of intentional sex discrimination, consisting of setting the wage scale for
female guards, but not for male guards, at a level lower than its
own survey of outside markets and the worth of the job warranted.[8]

Several other courts examined the comparable worth doctrine in
1981 and 1982 and reached the same conclusion, that is, Title VII
does not require employers to use job evaluation in setting wages,
but Title VII does require employers who use the job evaluation technique to apply it impartially to male and female jobs.[9] Then, in 1983,
a federal district court upheld a comparable worth suit brought by
the American Federation of State, County, and Municipal Employees
(AFSCME) against the State of Washington. The union charged that
despite a 1977 state legislative order calling for job evaluations for
state employees, Washington had persisted in allowing the market to
set wages. Supporting the validity of job evaluation, the court ruled
that Washington's actions violated Title VII. The state stood to pay
AFSCME's female employees as much as $1 billion in retroactive
compensation.[10]

However, on September 4, 1985, the Ninth Circuit Federal Court
of Appeals overturned the lower court's decision. "Neither law nor
logic deems the free market system a suspect enterprise," ruled Judge
Anthony Kennedy. "Title VII does not obligate [the State of
Washington] to eliminate an economic inequality it did not create."
AFSCME now plans to take its case to the Supreme Court.[11]

The sequence of events that led to Judge Kennedy's reversal followed
the standard pattern of comparable worth disputes at state and local
levels. First, under pressure from unions or other groups, legislators
mandate a job evaluation study for government employees. This study
becomes the basis for an attempt to carry out comparable worth, either
through a strike (as in the city of San Jose) or through a lawsuit charg-
ing discrimination, whether the employer used the job evaluation study
to set wages (as in the *Gunther* case) or not (as in the *AFSCME* case).
The plaintiffs in these cases have argued that comparable worth is
required by the Equal Pay Act and Title VII. Since most courts have
not been persuaded by this argument (*AFSCME v. State of Washington*
was a notable exception), pay equity advocates have tried to promote
new legislation that would explicitly require comparable worth. Now
that the Ninth Circuit Court's ruling has obstructed the judicial route,
advocates are likely to push even harder through legislative channels.

Sometimes, in response to lobbying by civil servants and women's groups, governments have simply legislated a pay increase for its female job titles voluntarily (as in Minnesota or Los Angeles).[12]

Comparable Worth in Congress

The current drive for comparable worth at the federal level is following a similar pattern. Bills that would require a study of wages in federal employment are pending in both the House (HR 3008, sponsored by Mary Rose Oakar [D.–Ohio], and the Senate (S 519, sponsored by Daniel Evans [R.–Washington].[13] Because these bills ask only for wage studies, they appear relatively innocuous, and so have an excellent chance of passing in Congress this term.[14] Obviously, it is too soon to know whether these studies would be used as the basis for lawsuits or further legislation requiring comparable worth at the federal level, but the language of other pending legislation suggests that the bill's sponsors hope to enact comparable worth directly in federal employment and indirectly in private employment.

Another bill, HR 375, which has 55 sponsors, directs the EEOC to "develop and implement a program to provide appropriate technical assistance to any *private or public* entity requesting such assistance to eliminate discriminating pay practices and implement the principle of *equal pay for jobs of equal value. . . .*" (emphasis added).[15] This clause redefines discrimination in comparable worth terms and clearly includes the private sector.

The Senate version of this particular bill (S 5)* is much more explicit. It states: "The Congress finds that . . . the Federal agencies charged with the responsibility for enforcement of Federal equal employment opportunity laws and directives have failed to take action, pursuant to applicable laws and directives, to seek to eliminate discriminatory wage-setting practices and discriminatory wage differentials."[16] In the context of the bill, this passage sounds as though comparable worth were already required by law and that the EEOC and the Justice Department have been negligent in not enforcing comparable worth standards. This language could easily be interpreted to require comparable worth in all areas under the reach of current discrimination law.

---

* See Appendix.

The bill also says that the purpose of the legislation is to help eliminate discriminatory wage differentials by:

(1) providing for the development and utilization of equitable job-evaluation techniques that will . . . help ensure that all employees, irrespective of sex, race, ethnicity, age or disability, receive comparable pay for work of comparable worth. . . .

(3) encouraging and stimulating public and private employers to eliminate discriminatory wage-setting practices and discriminatory wage differentials through the development and utilization of equitable job-evaluation techniques in setting wage rates.[17]

Thus, S 5 explicitly requires a comparable worth standard, names job evaluation as the appropriate wage-setting technique, and includes the private sector.

2. Political Support for Comparable Worth

TWO HIGHLY VISIBLE GROUPS HAVE been the driving political force behind comparable worth—women's rights organizations, especially the National Organization for Women (NOW), and organized labor, especially public employee unions. Apart from the principles at stake, each of these groups has something to gain by appealing to comparable worth's natural constituents.

The Women's Movement

The feminist movement has fallen on hard times. In its early days, progress was relatively easy because there were so many obvious things to correct—the right of married women to keep property in their own names, indeed to keep their own names; the right to abortion; the right to enter "male" occupations; the right to reenter the labor force or maintain a job after marriage. These battles, easy for many women to identify with, have been fought and won.

But lately, victories have been slower in coming, partly because the feminist movement's new causes are not as universally appealing to women. Government funding for abortions does not have the same powerful appeal as the right to choose abortion in the first place. Unisex insurance does not have the same impact on women's lives as equal pay for equal work. Government-funded day care is not a priority for women who have no children, nor are all women anxious to pay for it through higher taxes.

This means the women's movement has sought some new issues, issues with emotional impact and widespread appeal. Comparable worth is such an issue. It trades on the now famous "59 cents" that

11

women supposedly earned relative to every dollar men earned in 1977. (This issue will be addressed below.) In addition, because comparable worth focuses on higher wages for traditionally female jobs, it appeals to working-class women as well as to middle-class women.

This broader appeal is an important feature of pay equity politics. The women's movement has always had a difficult time winning support from working-class women. Most feminist leaders of the late '60s came from middle-class and professional families. (Betty Friedan's landmark work, *The Feminine Mystique,* originated with her survey of her classmates from Smith, an exclusive women's college.)[18] And the movement has naturally tended to reflect its founders' concerns, which often differed considerably from the concerns of women from blue collar families.

For example, the focus of the women's movement on doing the same work as men makes sense for women from middle-class or professional families. Most of the men in their lives do work that a woman is capable of performing, work that is intellectually demanding, but not physically taxing. These women can easily imagine themselves taking their places in the world of work, equal partners with their men.

The situation is quite different for the working-class woman. It is harder for her to imagine herself doing the more physically demanding work that the men in her life do. Comparable worth is one of the first women's issues that actually appeals to this group; after all, it promises higher pay for the jobs they are already doing.

Labor Unions

Comparable worth has also been embraced by organized labor. Initially, its endorsement might seem a bit odd, since unions have not until now considered women an important part of their constituency. In fact, after World War II, many industrial unions were instrumental in edging women out of the labor force to protect the jobs of their male membership.

But unions also have fallen on hard times. They have been losing elections more frequently—both representation elections, which allow a union to represent a group of workers, and decertification elections, in which already unionized workers vote to discontinue their union affiliation. Membership has steadily declined from 33.7 percent of the nonagricultural labor force in 1954, to 24 percent in 1978.[19] In the manufacturing sector, the traditional stronghold of unionism, the fraction of the unionized workforce fell from 32.2 percent in 1980 to 26.5 percent in 1984.[20] In short, unions need to find new sources of support.

By embracing comparable worth, unions attract women, a previously untapped resource, and also regain some of the moral high ground they used to occupy as defenders of the working class. They restore credibility to demands for wage increases in the name of equity.

Comparable worth has proven to be a particularly good cause for public employee unions, for two reasons. From the legal point of view, comparable worth can be more easily enacted in the public than the private sector. The government's legal right to regulate its own employment practices is beyond dispute. Governments can impose rules on themselves which may not survive constitutional challenges if imposed on private sector employers. Affirmative action, quotas and job set-asides, for example, have always been much more stringently enforced in the public sector and in businesses with government contracts, than in other businesses.[21]

From an economic point of view, the public sector is more fertile ground for comparable worth than the private sector. Unlike private sector companies, governments are not profit-seeking entities that thrive in a competitive setting by providing consumer goods and services at the lowest possible cost. Government employers will not go out of business or relocate if they are forced to pay higher than competitive wages. Public employee unions can pressure the legislature to enact job evaluations for state and local governments, and use the survey results to sue for higher wages. Often, the legislature will even appropriate money for the specific purpose of implementing pay equity. The increase in costs can of course be passed on to taxpayers. These are pay raises for the union's membership which would be more difficult to win any other way.

Unions and women's rights organizations, then, are staunch supporters of pay equity. Since both groups have traditionally been allied with the Democratic party, it is not surprising that the Democrats support comparable worth: most sponsors of the proposed federal legislation are Democrats. All three sponsors of the far-reaching S 5 are Democrats, as are five of the seven senators sponsoring S 519. The House bill requiring a comparable worth study of federal wages (HR 3008) has 107 sponsors, of whom 100 are Democrats. HR 375, which corresponds roughly to S 5, has only three Republicans out of fifty-five sponsors.[22]

Academics

Academics have become important participants in the comparable worth debate by providing evidence on the magnitude and causes of wage differentials and on the feasibility and accuracy of job evaluation. Scholars have testified before Congress and presented papers to the EEOC. Through these channels, the scholars who support comparable worth have given considerable credibility to legislation such as S 5 although they are generally more restrained in their proposals than their political counterparts. In fact, academic supporters differ among themselves as to how and to what extent comparable worth ought to be applied.

For example, Ruth Blumrosen, professor of management at Rutgers University, envisions a modest application of the comparable worth doctrine. In a roundtable discussion at the Manhattan Institute, a policy studies group, she remarked:

> I don't believe in comparable worth as a general concept. I want to make that very clear. I think the idea of relying on a job evaluation is a terrible idea. What I think we have to root out is systemic wage discrimination. . . . [I]f you look at situations where employers do use job evaluations, you have to determine whether they are applying them in a discriminatory fashion.[23]

Ray Marshall, secretary of labor under President Carter, writing with University of Texas economist Beth Palin, expressed a similarly restrained view in a report to the U.S. Civil Rights Commission:

> Comparable worth is a concept that is to be instituted at the level of the firm. Advocates of comparable worth do not ask that the government establish wage rates for the entire labor market or for any geographical region of that market. Comparable worth requires only that the firm's evaluation of jobs be unbiased and that pay scales be set up accordingly . . . the government's requirement is and should only be to see to it that whatever system the company uses not be discriminatory.[24]

Finally, the Committee on Occupational Classification and Analysis of the National Research Council and National Academy of Sciences states quite clearly at the end of its report on comparable worth:

It is important to note, however, that we do not recommend requiring the installation of a job evaluation plan in a firm not using one in an attempt to ensure that the firm's pay system is nondiscriminatory. At present we know of no method that would guarantee a "fair" pay system.[25]

The view expressed by these academics is essentially the view taken by the court in its *Gunther* decision, that is, that firms which currently use job evaluation should use it in an unbiased manner.

While some academics do support a more extensive application of comparable worth,[26] I am not aware of any academic who explicitly advocates anything as far reaching as S 5 or as national wage setting for the private sector. However, the moderate views of these academics are often used to support far more extensive policy proposals. The National Academy of Sciences report mentioned above, for instance, has been widely quoted in support of the comparable worth concept, more broadly defined.[27]

The views of most academics are restrained in comparison to the views of the political participants in the debate. This point is important because the academic advocates of comparable worth are probably the best informed about the likelihood of success of the various policy proposals. The political advocates of comparable worth have obviously gone beyond the most moderate of the academics, by introducing court challenges and legislation which go beyond the *Gunther* decision. NOW president Eleanor Smeal, for example, said in reference to HR 3008, which would require a job evaluation study of federal workers:

This study is a first step, but a necessary first step. We also intend to take this to the courts. We intend to take on the private sector. We intend to make this the political issue of the 1986 election.[28]

In California, a state task force on comparable worth issued a report requesting legislation to require private employers to implement comparable worth within their job pay systems.[29]

Thus, support for comparable worth comes from several quarters: the academy, public employee unions, NOW, and the Democratic party. Since each of these groups has somewhat different constituencies and interests, their proposals and strategies vary. Most of the discussion which follows will focus on the consequences of implementing comparable worth widely throughout the private sector.

3. Job Evaluation

NOW LET US TURN TO the nuts and bolts of comparable worth and examine the technique generally considered best adaptable to its purpose: job evaluation. As mentioned earlier, job evaluation has become one of the major sources of conflict in the comparable worth debate. Supporters believe that if companies used job evaluation techniques fairly they could eliminate the presumed sex bias in wage scales. Opponents maintain a more skeptical stance for a number of reasons.

How Job Evaluation Began

Consider the genesis of job evaluation. During the Second World War, many goods were controlled both in price and quantity. Government jobs, especially defense jobs, grew rapidly, and in many cases, there was no market mechanism by which to set wages—how much, for example, should the military pay drafted soldiers? The National War Labor Board (WLB) had the responsibility of setting wages in war related industries. Herbert Northrup, current chairman of the Labor Relations Council at the Wharton School and a former WLB hearing officer said:

> [Before the war] wage structures were frequently set in one plant operation without regard to another. The advent of unions and the experience of compulsory arbitration under the WLB tremendously changed this. Unions required that where skills were similar, there should be similar or equal pay. At the same time, the WLB was overwhelmed by the tasks of determining wage levels, effectuating

16

wage controls and settling new collective bargaining contracts, as well as by the complication of numerous disputes alleging individual wage inequities.[30]

The WLB used job evaluation to compare jobs because large parts of the market mechanism had been suspended due to wartime emergency. Because of these special circumstances, the usefulness of job evaluation techniques in wartime does not necessarily imply that the techniques would be equally successful when widely applied during more normal circumstances.

Evaluation of "Internal" Jobs

In recent years, private sector companies have used job evaluation surveys for two principal purposes—to set wages when no outside market exists for particular jobs (these are known as "internal" jobs) and to settle or forestall employee equity disputes.[31]

The first situation arises when an employee is hired at the entry level and advanced through the ranks within a firm. Trained internally, the employee acquires a great deal of knowledge and skill which is specific to that firm and of little use elsewhere. This individual's wages cannot be easily set by comparison with market wages, since there is no obvious market for the firm's specific skills. Accordingly, the firm may use some form of job evaluation to set wages for jobs of this kind.

But note that the company develops this plan by first considering other jobs in the firm, known as "key" jobs, which *do* have outside markets. Then, management, generally with help from consultants, creates a list of key job attributes, and correlates them with market wages to determine what each attribute is "worth." That is, the firm figures out how much wages are increased or decreased by each skill or job attribute. Once these "key" figures have been set, they are applied to the non-key, or internal jobs. The essence of this method is its reliance on the market.

Evaluation to Keep the Peace

Companies also use job evaluation to arbitrate employee equity disputes. In instances when consumer tastes or technology change,

some occupations simply become more valuable though the job content remains constant. Market considerations dictate higher wages to
workers in such occupations, even if internal equity does not. Management may use job evaluation to avoid the obvious morale problems
in these situations.

Take the growth of computer technology. As the cost of computers
falls, making them accessible to more companies, people with computer programming skills suddenly become in demand. Companies
are forced to pay these employees higher wages—regardless of internal equity considerations—or risk losing them.

Since the firm faces competition for its labor, its ability to use job
evaluation will be constrained by market forces. In fact, many scholars
argue that job evaluation merely serves a cosmetic purpose in settling equity disputes. A company sets up evaluation committees
primarily to persuade all its employees that the wages it is forced to
pay are fair.

Thus, job evaluation as currently practiced is a market-based technique. When firms use job evaluation to set wages for non-key jobs,
they rely on the market to do so. When firms use job evaluation to
mediate internal equity disputes, they are constrained by the market.

How Comparable Worth Fits In

Now the question is, how would comparable worth operate under this
system? Interestingly, the traditional women's jobs are not of the sort
that normally require job evaluation to set wages. Women's jobs are
both competitive and readily keyed to market wages. Vocations such
as nursing, secretarial work, or school teaching have wide lateral
mobility—until recently, women often chose the most portable jobs
in case their husbands' careers required a move.

But most pay equity advocates do not want to rely solely on the
market in setting wages. The essence of their argument is that market
wages are hopelessly riddled with discrimination. Therefore, using
the market to set wages, even with some form of job evaluation, may
not reduce the earnings gap between men and women.

The most moderate comparable worth advocates want to force companies which currently use job evaluation to use it fairly. The essence
of their argument is that even when characteristics of the job are ac-
counted for, as job evaluation purports to do, women are paid less
than they should be. That is, the same skill components receive lower

Figure 1: The Results of a Hypothetical Job Evaluation Study

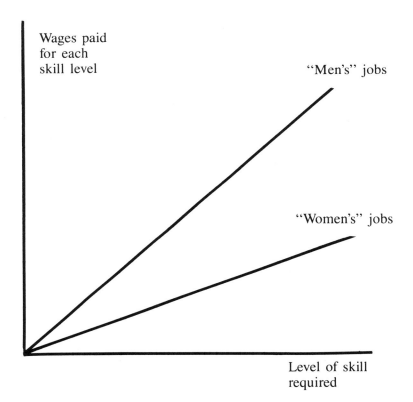

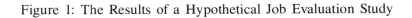

pay in women's jobs than other jobs. So applying the same job evaluation system to all employees would give women's jobs higher wages.

Figure 1 illustrates this argument. The horizontal axis measures the
skill level required for various job classifications. The "skill" measure
could be anything from formal education requirements to the level
of interpersonal or social skills required. The vertical axis measures
the wage level associated with each skill level. In general, a higher
wage would be associated with higher skill requirements as shown
by the two upward sloping lines in Figure 1. Such lines can be thought
of as rate tables or schedules showing the rates that employers must
pay for additional skill.

The line labeled "men's jobs" lies above the line "women's jobs" to represent the idea that men's jobs receive a higher wage at each level of skill than women's jobs of comparable skill. The moderate comparable worth advocates want to require that the skills in all jobs be compensated at the same rate. The precise rate is less important to these advocates than that the compensation schedules be equal. They would prefer that the payment schedule for men's jobs simply be applied to the women's jobs as well. However, there are obviously many lines lying between the two lines in Figure 1 that would pay the two types of jobs at the same rate, so presumably many different compensation schedules would be acceptable to these advocates.

When presented in this form, comparable worth seems like the simple rectification of an obvious injustice and appears to be relatively innocuous. Yet, there are problems with this argument. The primary use of most job evaluation systems is to set pay for non-key jobs. But it has already been pointed out that women's jobs are not generally in this category. Because the market for women's jobs is so competitive, job evaluation is generally not used to actually set wages. Firms simply let the market set wages. Nor is job evaluation ordinarily used to justify or rationalize the wages paid. Paying the "going rate" is its own justification. The clerical staff may be included in a company's job survey more for the sake of completeness than for actually using the survey to set wages.

In addition, firms often use different pay schedules for reasons that may have nothing to do with sex discrimination per se. Different payment schedules for skills may be used due to location differences, higher demand for skills in one industry than another, different union agreements, or the lack of a union, or for different occupational groupings. That is, if we compare jobs according to some of these other criteria, we often find different pay scales being used, even for jobs which are roughly all male. Figure 2 gives some illustrations. All of these factors are legitimate cost considerations that are quite separate from discrimination.[32]

Are there such cost considerations which might result in lower wage schedules for women's jobs? Perhaps the lower wages in the female dominated jobs exist due to large numbers of people willing to do those jobs. This cannot be described as discrimination unless people are forced into those jobs and restrained from other occupations. But if women choose those jobs because they are consistent with the other choices they are making, then a large supply of women to these jobs cannot be called discriminatory. Thus, comparable worth, even in its most limited definition of requiring job evaluation plans to be

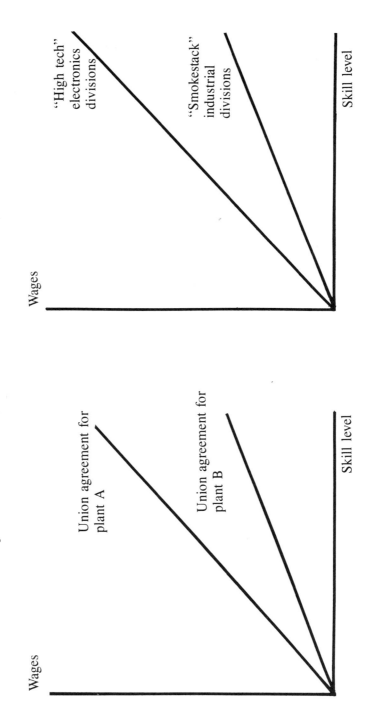

Figure 2: The Results of a Hypothetical Job Evaluation Study for a Corporation with Several Plants and Divisions

applied uniformly, may not be overcoming discrimination at all. Rather, it is paying more money to female-dominated jobs, regardless of whether these jobs are low paying due to discrimination, or due to other factors.

Some comparable worth advocates envision a more far-reaching application of the concept than simply requiring companies to use job evaluation fairly. Some idea of what these pay equity advocates envision can be seen by examining the work of Ronnie J. Steinberg, director of the Program on Comparable Worth at SUNY, Albany, and one of the chief investigators for the New York State comparable pay study.[33]

The first major issue has to do with the dependence of traditional job evaluation studies on market wages. If discrimination is embedded in market wages, then job evaluations based solely on the labor market will perpetuate that discrimination. Steinberg suggests several statistical procedures for removing the impact of discrimination on the job evaluation process she would like to use to set wages. This seems to place her squarely in the camp of those who simply want to insure that job evaluations are applied fairly to all.

There is more to the story, though. Part of the problem that Steinberg sees is that the job evaluations contain an additional source of bias, beyond the fact that they are based on biased market wages. She argues that most job evaluation studies are biased in the kinds of skills they survey and measure. Skills required in female jobs are often not specified in as much detail. Hence, women's jobs are undervalued.

> When examining why the differences emerged, the researchers found that the Labor Department had overlooked important characteristics of the female-dominated jobs, especially those associated with taking care of children. The evaluators did not regard these as job-related *skills,* but rather as *qualities intrinsic to being a woman.* In other words, the job evaluators were confusing the content and responsibilities of a paid job with stereotypic notions about the characteristics of the job holder.[34]

In Steinberg's view, two separate corrections must be made. First, the job evaluation survey itself must become unbiased by enumerating the skills associated with female and male jobs. Second, these skills must be correlated with market wages which have been corrected for discriminatory bias.

This is easier said than done. As Steinberg goes on to point out:

. . . [S]tudy results are highly sensitive to which jobs are studied, what information is contained within the job descriptions, what factors are emphasized and in what weighting, and how the factors have been scaled. I am not saying that one must abandon these methodologies. Rather, I am suggesting that there are better ways to conduct this research.[35]

Unfortunately she does not elaborate.

Any job evaluation study necessarily contains many judgment calls, as Steinberg's comments attest.[36] And there is no independent standard by which these decisions can be judged. Therein lies the difference between the use of job evaluation in comparable worth studies and its use for more traditional purposes. The traditional use of job evaluation is to duplicate the market wage setting process for jobs which have no obvious market. The many judgments about what factors to include and so forth can be measured against a clear standard, namely how well these decisions duplicate existing market wages.

The trouble with using job evaluation studies for comparable worth is that once the market standard has been discarded, there is no useful replacement for it. Discrimination is not a well-defined standard because the wage differentials, even "unexplained" differentials, do not measure the exact magnitude of discrimination. (This issue will be addressed below.) So decisions about which job traits to include, and how to scale and rank them, will necessarily be arbitrary. A wide variety of results is possible, depending upon the structure of the study, and there is no objective way to choose among them. Thus, making job evaluations "fair" is really not as straightforward a proposition as some pay equity advocates would like to believe. As Professor Donald P. Schwab of the University of Wisconsin–Madison, has observed:

Job evaluation can undoubtedly be used to accomplish the objectives of comparable worth advocates. After all, it is an inherently subjective technique. Just as it can be manipulated to scale jobs consistent with the external market (as currently done by firms), it can be manipulated to scale jobs to ameliorate gender-related wage differentials (as advocates want). . . . Job evaluation does not produce equity in some objective, scientific way; job evaluation helps achieve whatever criterion of equity its administrators desire.[37]

4. The Trouble with Numbers

PROPONENTS OF COMPARABLE WORTH DRAW from two statistical sources for their assumption that women continue to be discriminated against in the job market: the aggregate earnings data compiled by the U.S. Census department, and the findings of social scientists using what are known as cross-section studies. These numbers should be carefully examined before asserting the need for a corrective policy such as comparable worth.

The 59 Cents Fallacy

The emblem that first gave comparable worth its political punch was a simple green and white button bearing the Equal Rights Amendment (ERA) slogan "59 cents." In the memorable words of Judy Goldsmith, past president of NOW:

> Nothing better illustrates the economic plight of American women than NOW's 59 cents campaign button. . . . The plain frightening fact [is] that most women are paid just over half as much as men for the very same work—to be exact, 59 cents for every dollar earned by a man.

This gap widened between 1955, when women's earnings averaged 64 percent of men's, and 1977, when the level dropped to 59 percent where, as we have said, it held until 1980.[38] In Goldsmith's opinion, echoed by Eleanor Smeal, the current president of NOW, and other feminist leaders, the wage differential clearly signalled greater job discrimination.

24

But how could this be? Women have many more opportunities now than their mothers ever dreamed of. They can attend the military service academies, divinity schools, and all of the Ivy League colleges. There are women on the space shuttle, in the pulpits of many churches, and on the faculties of Ivy League schools. Census data indicate that the number of women employed as managers and administrators jumped from 1 million in 1970 to 2.6 million by 1979. The number of female lawyers and judges rose during this period from 13,182 to 61,000.[39] The *New York Times* recently reported that the number of women holding bachelor's degrees in engineering rose from 744 in 1974 to 10,761 in 1984.[40] And whereas many of our mothers and grandmothers were forced to give up their jobs not only when they became pregnant but even when they got married, most married women and mothers may now keep working irrespective of need.

In short, it seems unlikely that women actually face more discrimination today than a generation ago. It would be particularly absurd for a feminist to concede defeat after twenty years of obvious progress. But if women do not face more discrimination today than in the 1950s, and still the earnings gap widened, how do we explain this curious phenomenon?

First, is the 59 cents figure still accurate? No—the gap has narrowed in recent years, from 60 percent in 1980 to 62 percent in 1982. Second, consider what these numbers refer to. They represent an aggregate—the ratio of full-time, year-round female workers' average earnings to those of full-time, year-round male workers, in all civilian industries and professions.[41] The aggregate figure does not correct for age, experience, marital status, education, or measures of job skill, nor does it take into account changes in the composition of the work force.

Yet the most striking fact about the job market since 1950 is how many more women it now contains—over two-and-a-half times as many in 1982 (47 million) than in 1950 (17.8 million). The labor force participation rate (that is, the percentage of women who are working or seeking work) jumped from 31 percent in 1952 to 52 percent in 1982, while the male rate remained roughly constant.[42] Since increases in supply are usually associated with declines in price, this rise in the number of employed women may well have caused a fall in women's wages relative to men's.

Many readers may be not persuaded that the labor market follows these simple laws of supply and demand. Fair enough. Consider another instance in which relative wages fell, one that cannot possibly be attributed to discrimination. The baby boom created a huge bulge in the supply of young workers entering the labor force in the late 1960s, relative to the number of older, more experienced workers. And the earnings of these younger workers as a percentage of the earnings of older workers was 63 percent in 1968, but only 54 percent in 1974. That is, a young individual who entered the labor force in 1968 earned a weekly wage which was 63 percent of that earned by middle-aged, experienced adult workers, but a similar young individual who entered the labor force in 1974 earned only 54 percent of the of adult workers. Wages fell for entry level jobs because the baby boomers were competing among themselves.[43]

The increase in the number of women in the work force took place much more gradually than the increase in supply of young baby boom workers. And the accompanying fall in relative wages was much less severe for women workers relative to men workers than for young workers relative to older workers. On the basis of this evidence, some economists have been surprised that the earnings gap between men and women didn't widen even further than it did.[44]

Probably the reason the gap did not widen further is that not all the women entering the labor force went into "female" jobs (see Table 3). Many entered jobs and professions formerly closed to women in which they compete primarily with men and not with other women. Because they were not increasing the supply of workers to female jobs, the women who pioneered in the fields of banking, medicine, construction, and law did not lower the average wages of women.

Despite this, however, a disproportionate number of them entered the traditionally female jobs. Clerical jobs actually account for the same fraction of the jobs held by women today as in 1960.[45] In addition, most of the new entrants have been older women, returning to work after childrearing or entering the labor force for the first time. These women, whose labor force participation in many ways represents a success of the women's movement, had much less experience than the average woman already in the labor force. They also tended to be less educated than average. The result is that the average skill level of women in the labor force fell, despite the increases in education levels of women overall. The older women entering the labor force pulled down the average skill levels of women workers.

A recent study that broke down the earnings gap by age shows that strong wage gains have been made by younger women in the last few

Table 3
Increases in Female Participation in Male-Dominated Jobs

(Women Workers as a Percent of all Workers
for Selected Occupations, 1972 and 1982)

	1972	1982
Accountants	21.7	38.6
Computer Specialists	16.8	28.5
Engineers	0.8	5.7
Lawyers & Judges	3.8	15.4
Life and Physical Scientists	10.0	20.6
Personnel & Labor Relations Workers	31.0	49.6
Physicians, Dentists & Related Practitioners	9.3	14.6
Social Scientists	21.3	38.0
College & University Teachers	28.0	35.4
Engineering & Science Technicians	9.1	18.3
Bank Officers & Financial Managers	19.0	37.1
Buyers, Wholesale & Retail Trade	32.9	43.1
Insurance Agents, Brokers & Underwriters	11.6	26.2
Real Estate Agents & Brokers	36.7	50.2
Stock & Bond Sales Agents	9.9	19.8
Sales Representatives, Manufacturing Industries	6.8	21.4

Source: Statistical Abstract of the U.S., 1984, Table Number: 696, p. 419.

years. Women twenty-five to thirty-four years old received 69 percent of men's wages in 1980 and 73 percent by 1983. Women twenty
to twenty-four years old earned 78 percent of what men their age earned
in 1980, and by 1983 this ratio had risen to 86 percent. Some resear-
chers expect the earnings gap to narrow fairly rapidly now that the
influx of older women has slowed. The majority of women entering
the job market today are younger, better educated, and have strong
labor force attachments (that is, a long-term commitment to their jobs),
which undoubtedly explains why the aggregate earnings gap narrowed
to 64 percent in 1983,[46] and has probably continued to diminish in
the last two years.

Clearly, then, it is folly for comparable worth advocates to presume that discrimination explains the aggregate wage differentials. The "59 cents" fallacy should be put to rest. It is necessary to look elsewhere for proof of discrimination.

Cross-Section Studies, or What You Don't Know Hurts You

Cross-section studies are often held up as a more sophisticated means by which to measure discrimination than aggregate earnings data. These studies examine wage disparities between large groups of men and women at a particular moment in time. A researcher typically looks for relevant characteristics such as age, education, occupation, marital status, work history, and union status. Some studies also try to weigh attributes that make a job more or less desirable—hence more or less difficult to fill at a given wage—such as the location and nature of the industry it serves, whether it requires physical exertion, or entails exposure to environmental hazards such as pollution or toxic chemicals. The researcher then attempts to statistically calculate the effect of all these factors on wages, and attributes any residual earnings differential to discrimination.[47]

Cross-section study results have reduced the aggregate earnings gap between men and women by roughly one half. Thus the extent of the problem diminishes, but discrimination remains an issue, since an earnings difference between the sexes of about 20 percent remains.[48]

But must this residual wage disparity be considered a function of discrimination? Consider a population of white men. Cross-section studies that attempt to explain wage variations among white males using measurable factors such as education and age are able to account for only about 40 to 50 percent.[49] In other words, these factors account for less than half of the earnings differences among a population of white men. Yet no one would necessarily conclude that the men with lower earnings had been discriminated against.

The problem with cross-section studies is that many things influence earnings but are not readily measured. Work habits, job commitment, personality traits, leadership qualities, willingness to assume responsibility, and other intangibles affect an individual's earning power. Residual variations might also result from things like good luck, bad luck, being in the right place at the right time or vice versa, family and social connections or the lack thereof.[50]

So it seems quite likely that residual earnings disparities are not really an index of discrimination; in fact, the possibility that there is no discrimination whatsoever cannot be ruled out. Unmeasurable factors account for some 60 percent of the variation in white male earnings, while unexplained earnings differences between the sexes amount to somewhere between 13 and 34 percent. So it is possible that men and women have widely different amounts of unmeasured characteristics, at least enough so that if they could be measured, there might be no significant wage differential at all.

Strictly speaking, the opposite possibility cannot be ruled out either—that women actually have *more* unmeasured productivity traits, but face so much discrimination that they are paid less despite greater productivity. Either way, cross-section earnings data appear to be inherently inconclusive; they measure the magnitude of our ignorance as much as anything else.

Conclusion

Thus, labor force discrimination is a problem of unknown and probably unknowable magnitude. Neither the aggregate statistics nor the cross-section studies are able to perfectly separate earnings differences that arise due to discrimination from earnings differences that arise due to other factors. Unfortunately, comparable worth focuses squarely on these flawed measures of discrimination. Comparable worth asks policymakers to make precise wage adjustments to correct for a problem of unknown size.

5. The Impact of Marriage and Children on Women's Earnings

IN THEIR EAGERNESS TO MARSHAL evidence of wage discrimination, proponents of comparable worth often underplay the most significant "number" of all: the fact that never-married women earn much more than women who have been married—essentially the same amount as never-married men. This pattern has been observed at least since the 1960s. Controlling for marital status alone closes nearly all of the earnings gap, without reference to occupation, education, or any other factors. The question is, what is so different about marriage?[51]

The obvious answer is that married women tend to have children, and at least until recently, assumed most of the responsibility for raising them. This usually entails (and certainly in the past it almost always did entail) leaving the labor force to care for children, either for a short or long time. And this absence from the labor force has important economic consequences that have nothing to do with discrimination.

The Need for Portable Skills

First of all, women, particularly working-class women, lose time and hence experience because of family responsibilities. The average working-age woman has less labor force experience overall than a man her age, and less time on her current job, so she obviously earns less money.[52] There is a more subtle effect as well. If a woman expects to marry and raise children, she will often choose a job that allows for relatively easy movement in and out of the labor force; a job for which the required skills do not atrophy with disuse or become quickly obsolete.[53]

Thus a woman who wants to teach is more likely to become a primary school teacher than a college professor. College professors must do research, and new developments in their fields may come about rapidly. Similar arguments can be made for doctors in comparison with nurses and paramedical personnel and for lawyers in comparison with legal secretaries and paralegals.

The Loss of Human Capital

To illustrate, imagine a woman who runs a real estate business. She started working as a real estate agent right after college, and by her late twenties had her own small agency. Now in her early thirties, she wants to start a family. She would like to spend five years or so raising children.

Because she is self-employed, discrimination is not an issue. How many hours she works, when she works, how much she gets paid—these decisions are all up to her since she is not at the mercy of an employer. She simply will not earn as much in commissions if she works fewer hours. No one is to blame. She has chosen family time over a higher income.

So suppose she does quit altogether for five years. She will lose more than five years' worth of income. She will also lose some of the human capital she invested in building her business. Her local real estate market will change over the course of five years, and she will probably have missed many of the changes. She may become rusty at closing sales. She may have to become reaquainted with many of the new players in the market or with new types of mortgages. In short, her human capital will depreciate.

The consequences of this depreciation are magnified over the five years she is out of the labor force in comparison with the situation of her male counterparts. Far from letting their capital deteriorate, they have been adding to their stock of knowledge and experience.

Thus women have traditionally chosen certain fields precisely because the skills those fields require do not atrophy or depreciate as greatly as do those needed for many male-dominated fields; these fields make sense in the larger context of their lives.

New Problems, New Solutions

Unfortunately, the attributes that made women's jobs appealing in the past are the very attributes which limit financial benefits like opportunities for advancement, new challenges, or more money. Now that women must place greater emphasis on financial rewards than on flexibility, more are entering male occupations. In 1950, men's income was the sole source of income in 70 percent of American households; in 1984, less than 15 percent of households depended solely on the wages of a working male.[54] The higher probability of divorce also means that more women will become sole supporters of their families at some point.

As women acquire skills that atrophy, they confront problems their mothers' generation never faced. Some work part-time in their old jobs once their children are born. Others temporarily leave their employers to start their own consulting firms, which allows them more flexibility and safeguards their human capital until they are ready to return to work full-time.[55] Moreover, many of the male professions mentioned above, college professor, doctor, lawyer, have the potential advantage of offering more flexible work schedules. Now that fewer women are leaving the full-time labor force for marriage and motherhood many of them are beginning to choose the professions and take advantage of these possibilities while their children are young.

And of course, some women never leave the labor force. Daycare, now an $8 billion annual industry, is expected to grow twofold by 1990.[56] And these figures do not include children cared for in private homes, by neighbors, grandparents, or through other informal arrangements.[57]

In sum, women's job choices are no longer primarily dictated by the need to drop out of the labor force when they begin a family. This change surely contributes to the recent gain in women's relative earnings. But so long as women take more time out of the labor force than men, some earnings difference will probably continue to exist. This would hold true even in the absence of discrimination.

6. The Economic Consequences of Comparable Worth

TRYING TO PINPOINT WAGE DISCRIMINATION and administer corrective measures through existing techniques such as job evaluation presents numerous problems. Still, if improving women's economic status is a worthy goal, these theoretical problems and technical hurdles should not make us reject comparable worth. If, on the other hand, comparable worth does not achieve these objectives, if it would leave a host of worse problems in its wake, then it is time to discard this policy altogether. An analysis of the economic consequences of adopting comparable worth to raise women's wages on a large scale in both the public and private sectors—for it is naive to suppose that comparable worth would not soon be adapted to more general purposes—may make it easier to decide on the value of comparable worth as a solution to women's employment problems.

Fewer Jobs

If comparable worth became the law of the land, it would result in raising the wages of traditionally female jobs above the market rate. Higher wages for traditionally female occupations would represent an increased cost to private employers, which no proposed legislation calls for providing funds to offset. The employer's likely response would be to reduce the number of job openings in the traditionally female fields. Many secretarial and clerical functions, for example, can be performed with fewer employees and more technology, such as word processors and answering machines. Managers might be asked to type their own letters, answer their own phones, and let one secretary handle the correspondence and messages for a group. The more effective comparable worth is in raising wages, the greater the incentive for employers to use these techniques to reduce the number of jobs. This could take the form of actual layoffs, but would be more apt to take place through attrition or slower rates of employment growth.

Another likely consequence is that higher wages will induce women to behave differently. More will be attracted to a reduced number of traditionally female jobs now calling for higher pay. So artificially high wages will increase the number of unemployed women. This argument may sound familiar to some readers, because it is often made against minimum wage. In essence, comparable worth is tantamount to a higher minimum wage for women's jobs, set higher than the minimum for other jobs.[58]

In addition to the usual problems caused by the minimum wage, comparable worth will create two other problems for women. There will be greater competition for women's jobs. And women's jobs will probably become more rigidly segregated.

More Competition

Two groups of women will be lured into traditionally female jobs by the higher wages offered by comparable worth; those who would otherwise be out of the labor force and some of those who would otherwise have gone into traditionally male jobs. Women entering the labor force in the hope of obtaining one of the newly higher paid women's jobs are likely to be disappointed, since those now scarce jobs are more likely to go to women with the most experience and best credentials. A woman returning to work hoping to gain labor force experience is the least likely to land one of these jobs. In effect, comparable worth will close many doors to homemakers entering the work force with little or no labor market experience.

On the other hand, some of the women drawn into the traditionally female jobs will be drawn away from the jobs that have traditionally been regarded as male jobs, because comparable worth increases the wages of "women's" jobs relative to the wages of "men's" jobs. This is just another way of saying that the relative gain for women from entering one of the male dominated fields declines for women. So comparable worth actually reduces the incentive for women to leave the traditionally female jobs and enter the fields that have, up until now, been considered male bastions.

Some feminists argue that working-class and lower middle-class women would benefit most from comparable worth. Most of the gains in male dominated occupations have come in the white collar professions, rather than in the blue collar crafts and trades (see Table 3). Wives and daughters of blue collar workers may find it more difficult to obtain the education necessary for the male dominated professions. Or they may simply be uncomfortable doing jobs that are not only unusual for women, but which are unusual for the men in their lives as well. Becoming a white collar professional would make these women more like their husbands' bosses than like their husbands. Surely, the argument goes, comparable worth is the only realistic hope for these women ever receiving higher wages.

But not all children of the working class are constrained to do as their parents did. Many working class parents are eager for their children to become more educated and professional than themselves, despite the fact they may have very ambivalent feelings about it when it actually happens. However, once a young women has made career and marriage choices which are similar to those of her parents, it certainly will be difficult for her to shift gears and move into the male dominated white collar occupations.

Women from working-class families, moreover, would probably benefit *least* from comparable pay for female occupations. Since the competition for these occupations will be increased, women of average intelligence and skills entering the labor force expecting to pursue a traditional female occupation are likelier to be disappointed. A smaller number of more lucrative jobs will go to those with the most experience and best credentials. Working-class women will be competing with the women who might otherwise have pursued "male" jobs.

Finally, the simplest way to raise the wages of the female dominated jobs that working-class women so often do is to decrease the supply of labor to those jobs. We ought to encourage those women who face fewer constraints to enter the non-traditional fields. Women from professional families are not as likely as working-class women to outdistance their husbands and fathers by becoming investment bankers rather than bank tellers. They do not have to leave everything familiar to them in order to enter male-dominated professions, as working-class women must if they enter such jobs. And finally, more intelligent women of any family background are better able to take advantage of the wider range of occupational choices now open to women.

Yet, at least until recently, there has been little correlation between intelligence and occupational achievement for women, although that correlation has been quite strong for men. In a now classic early study, two-thirds of the women with genius-level IQs of 170 or above were occupied as housewives or office workers.[59] Even given the flaws of IQ tests, society's failure to challenge these women is a national disgrace, far worthier of a slogan than "59 cents."

Imagine yourself an average woman, of about average intelligence and family background, applying for a job as a salesclerk at a department store. Does it really help you to be competing with women with genius-level IQs or a degree from Vassar? You may be sure that men who apply for jobs as truck drivers seldom face comparable competition. There is a very real sense then in which the traditional women's jobs are crowded with people who have no business being there.

Paying higher salaries for traditional women's jobs does nothing to ease the competition faced by working-class women. It does nothing to encourage the women who are socially or intellectually less constrained to move out of these jobs. To the contrary, pay equity does quite the opposite. It encourages women to choose the traditional jobs. In addition, by requiring higher than competitive wages, it gives employers an incentive to hire women with more impressive credentials. Comparable worth will result in fewer working-class women entering the jobs that are often their only reasonable option.

More Job Segregation

Some comparable pay advocates argue that because higher wages attracted men to women's jobs, a resulting decrease in job segregation would ultimately benefit women. Sex discrimination and occupational stereotypes, it is claimed, would become a thing of the past. That has to be conceded as one possibility. But the likelier result is that an influx of male competitors would merely offset the larger number of female applicants, some of whom might have chosen men's jobs. Besides, plenty of male occupations already pay more than women's jobs—the very impetus behind comparable worth—so why would men choose to be pioneers any more than women? All of these developments could add up to greater occupational sex segregation, not less.

Feminists who say they want to apply pay equity only to female-dominated sectors of the economy lend public support to the notion that some jobs are and always will be women's jobs. Isolating these jobs for special treatment institutionalizes the stereotypical notions about which jobs are women's jobs.

This point was dramatized for me during the "comparable worth" strike by Yale University's clerical and technical workers union, a predominantly female union, at an information meeting sponsored by some union supporters. One of my colleagues from the economics department was explaining statistical comparisons he had made between Yale's male and female employees. This particular professor was actually very sympathetic to the union's claim that the university was discriminating against its female workers. As a passing comment, he said that he did not have all the data he would have liked to have, and that in particular, it would have been better if he could have controlled for whether a person had a degree in the sciences. The reaction of that predominantly pro-comparable worth audience was to boo him.

At the time I was stunned (and I suspect my colleague was a bit surprised as well). But I realize in retrospect that I shouldn't have been surprised. That audience was saying that science degrees should not be considered intrinsically "worth" more than humanities degrees. They were saying that it is implicitly sexist to give greater rewards for science degrees, which men tend to pursue far more often than women. In effect, they were giving up on the early feminist goal of integrating women into science—a traditionally male field.

If a sizable group of younger women are still choosing the traditional jobs, perhaps it is precisely because they are traditional. Women have a thousand role models for female occupations; they do not have to face the uncomfortable problems of being the boss, they do not have to figure out how to give male subordinates orders. In short, traditional jobs are psychologically safe.

Perhaps comparable worth advocates have these psychological "barriers to entry" in mind when they argue that women are forced into traditional jobs. After all, women's upbringing and experience simply have not equipped them to compete aggressively in an all-male environment. Moreover, women with "men's" jobs may feel uncomfortable for a variety of reasons. Sometimes, because of a lack of role models or experience, they do not know how to act. More often, the men they work with do not know how to act in a respectful manner. Certain conversations stop when women approach. They are not included in the informal socializing, like golf and raquetball games, that make men in a profession part of a "network." In these situa-

tions, women naturally feel they must struggle just to be taken seriously. So it is hardly surprising that many women, aware of these problems through experience and hearsay, avoid these problems altogether
by choosing traditional jobs. Others get "burned out" from trying
to advance through a seemingly impassable thicket of male mores
and norms and stay in a holding pattern.

These barriers seem to amount to a powerful case for comparable
worth. The truth is that they do not. Paying more for the traditional
female jobs does not make it any easier for women to venture further
afield. It does not help correct sexist attitudes. It does not familiarize
us with the presence of women in powerful places. And it clearly
does not reduce the expectation that women belong in subordinate
roles. Rather, it exaggerates all the problems the women's movement
has been trying to change.

A case can be made that comparable worth has not created such
dire problems in places where it has already been carried out. But
the evidence is far from overwhelming. Comparable worth has only
been enacted relatively recently and on a piecemeal basis. It is too
soon to observe large numbers of people making lifetime career plans
or career changes as a result of a policy that is only a few years old.
More important, comparable worth so far has only been enacted in
the public sector. State and local governments, as I have already noted,
are not subject to the same competitive pressures as private sector
firms. In fact, most of the legislation requiring comparable worth actually appropriates tax money to meet the increased payroll costs. So
public sector employers are not as likely to reduce employment opportunities rapidly due to comparable worth. Thus, evaluating current comparable worth programs in the public sector as an example
of what would take place in the private sector is highly questionable.
Enacting comparable worth in the private sector will have all of the
economic problems I have described.

7. Social Problems

PAY EQUITY ADVOCATES ARGUE THAT women cluster in low-paying occupations because they never expected to be anything other than nurses or secretaries. They did not prepare themselves, either technically or psychologically, for other jobs. So they are "forced" into these jobs by their past, whether or not male employers continue to discriminate against them.

Displaced Housewives

That argument really applies only to women who are now roughly thirty-five years old and older. They began their lives expecting future husbands to meet their financial needs in exchange for homemaking. They never expected to be the sole source of financial support for themselves and their children, and they made educational and training plans accordingly. Their marriage "contracts" asked them to risk being economically dependent, but they were compensated by assurances that divorce was unlikely, and if by chance they did divorce, they would receive adequate alimony.

What happened to this group of women? A social revolution took place in the course of their lifetimes. Women were urged to break out of traditional social and economic roles. Many women began to feel that the roles of wife and mother were not enough to satisfy them for a lifetime. More and more women entered the labor force. The priorities for women shifted from house-bound domestic work and concerns to personal self-fulfillment, more education, and new opportunities outside the home. Divorce became more common, alimony payments less generous.

These changes are generally considered positive and healthy. But the older women now working out of necessity are one of society's most vulnerable groups. They were not entirely in a position to take advantage of the new freedom opened by the social revolution of the sixties and seventies. They had children and no job skills. Many of them were divorced and left to fend for themselves and their children. They literally had the rug pulled out from under them.

These are the women who are truly constrained labor market participants. They were forced into low-paying jobs by their lack of training and the circumstance of being caught in the middle of a major social upheaval that could not possibly have been foreseen and which upset all expectations. This group of women has the strongest claim on our sympathy and on our attention in the formation of public policy.

It might appear that the plight of this older group makes a strong case for some kind of comparable worth policy. But as we have already demonstrated, with fewer available jobs for a larger pool of applicants, companies would probably not choose displaced homemakers to fill them. Even if comparable worth could be targeted exclusively toward older women, it would reduce still the incentive for younger women to enter male jobs. "Don't worry, dear," might run the new version of a familiar refrain, "after the kids are grown, you can always get a job as a librarian. It pays well and it's such a nice job for a lady."

The simpler, more direct solution to the problem of displaced homemakers would be for divorce courts to recognize their special status. In the past, courts traditionally awarded these women generous alimony and child-support payments, as well as fair property settlements. Now much of this "favored" treatment has gone by the wayside—a casualty of the sexual revolution. Of the 17 million divorced women in this country, 85 percent receive no alimony at all. Furthermore, one study found that men's standard of living increased 72 percent the first year after a divorce, while women's with children drops 42 percent.[60]

The women's movement must take at least partial responsibility for this unfortunate situation. In its early days, the movement actively disapproved of alimony; it was seen as a tender trap that kept women dependent on men. Newly practicing women lawyers were so adamant about women's place in the work force that they worsened housewives' plight even more by seeking smaller settlements than they might have. The early feminists also argued for loosening divorce laws and encouraging women not to settle for mediocre or miserable marriages. Yet, the rise of no fault divorce, while making it easier for a woman to divorce, has also made it easier for a man to divorce his homemaker wife, leaving her to fend for herself financially. "In fault cases, twenty years ago, the tradition was one third of the husband's income to the wife. In the old days, you had this barter. The faulting party had to give something in order to get the divorce. . . . No fault benefits the faulting party," according to Circuit Court Judge Leander Foley of Milwaukee, a professor of law at Marquette University.[61]

Today there are two very different kinds of marriage contracts, and divorce in each case should be handled quite differently. For "traditional" marriages, in which the husband agrees to support his wife for life while she cares for the children, large divorce settlements should compensate her for the risk she took in not acquiring job skills. This potential monetary penalty would reduce the husband's incentive to divorce his wife during middle age—at the height of his earning power and her economic and social vulnerability.

In many "modern" marriages, where both partners work and share child care responsibilities—or perhaps, have no children at all, the woman is not as financially vulnerable. In the event of divorce, she is in a position to take care of at least herself and perhaps her children too. Divorce can and should be relatively easy; alimony payments could be relatively small. Dividing joint property should not be too difficult, since both partners contributed to the household's cash flow.

Social Arguments for Comparable Worth

Another argument for raising women's wages is that it will prompt people to take women more seriously: higher pay, even for the same job, means greater respect. This theory appeals to our common sense notion that "you get what you pay for." If you pay more for an employee, he or she is clearly more valuable.

We have already pointed out that a higher wage for a particular job will induce employers to hire fewer workers in that position. The employer will certainly hire the most qualified worker possible. And the mere fact that fewer workers are being hired means that each of them will be assigned to the most important and valuable tasks. So the higher wage might cause women's work to be more highly valued, but only because fewer women will be hired. Comparable worth will raise average productivity and earnings but only by eliminating the lower end of the earnings distribution.

But more to the point, is it really true that higher pay automatically means more respect? Teachers and clergy are highly "valued" and respected, but their jobs have never been particularly lucrative. On the other hand, municipal workers like garbagemen have been well paid since the advent of public employee unions, but their jobs have not particularly risen in public esteem. If anything, garbagemen have probably become the butt of more jokes since their salaries rose. Lawyers, politicians, and union leaders are hardly badly paid, yet they consistently receive low ratings in public opinion polls.

Of all the arguments in favor of comparable worth, surely the most damaging to women in the long run is that they need more income now that so many are single parents. It is puzzling to hear feminists today espouse this line. The "family responsibilities" argument—bitterly opposed by the women's movement in earlier days—drags us back to the fifties and before, when good jobs were reserved for family men and women were forced to quit their jobs when they married. Just as the fact that a man "has a family to support" ought not to justify paying him more than a single person, a woman's parental status should not be relevant to the wages her employer offers. Family responsibilities may well bear on the wages someone is willing to accept, but that is a separate issue. The argument of "need" undermines the feminist belief in work as a means of personal fulfillment. Even if a woman does not "need" the income, she can have a legitimate desire for satisfying work outside the home.

Finally, many comparable worth advocates say that the reason we need this policy is because neither Title VII nor the Civil Rights Act of 1964 have been adequately enforced to produce the necessary changes. The question, then, is why not? Because the government is not committed to the program? Because businesses find ways to evade the law? The next question is, why is comparable worth likely to be enforced more effectively? Why institute a new program rather than try to better enforce the old ones?

A Plea for Choice

The true goal of women's liberation today ought to be to help women obtain the fullest range of options consistent with their abilities and desires. A woman who wants a career should be supported in that decision. A woman who chooses to be a full-time housewife should be supported by the women's movement in that role. Women who wish to do both, either simultaneously or at different times in their lives, should be encouraged.

But each choice should be made with full awareness of the costs involved. It must be recognized that childrearing is very demanding. It also must be recognized that success in the world of work requires a substantial commitment of time and effort. And it must be recognized that dropping out of the labor force reduces lifetime earnings potential. Women have been exposed to enough public discussion of their options to be aware of these tradeoffs. It is increasingly unrealistic these days to maintain that women under thirty-five are forced into being secretaries and nurses and elementary school teachers. They must have read or heard or seen that taking clerical jobs would not make them chairman of the board someday. Young women who marry at an early age and take a "woman's" job to supplement the family income must also be regarded as having made a conscious choice.

Conclusion

These then, are my objections to comparable worth. It is a policy that abandons many of the noblest of the early feminist goals. Because it focuses only on those in traditionally female jobs, it essentially abandons the goal of integrating women fully into all sectors of the economy. By raising wages to the point that only those with the most skill and experience will be hired, it will reduce opportunities for homemakers who want to return to the labor force, and particularly for those displaced homemakers who must return. (Many of these women are in dire straits through no choice or fault of their own, and comparable worth creates problems for them while helping only those who have been fortunate enough to find employment.) Comparable worth will increase unemployment among women.

By arguing that more women need money now because more support families, comparable worth advocates reduce the legitimacy of married women working outside the home. The whole campaign for comparable worth shores up gender stereotypes by preserving and even glorifying stereotypical female jobs. It is similar to arguing that blacks are segregated into shining shoes and scrubbing floors, so that raising the wages of those jobs is the only fair thing to do.

Those who argue for comparable worth do so because they believe that the earnings differences between men and women are evidence that women are discriminated against and in need of special intervention or protection. I believe that these advocates have lost sight of the significance of the women's movement.

The point of the movement is for women to make their own life choices, with a minimum of constraints, including constraints imposed by government. To be sure, some women do not have the luxury of a wide range of choice and many other women make their choice on the basis of inadequate or erroneous information. Deplorable though this state of affairs may be, it does not call for government intervention. To the contrary, government should not interfere in the realm of individuals making their personal choices. Yet it is precisely these matters of personal choice and preference that confound our judgments about earnings differences between the sexes. Such differences could be evidence of different choices—or of different relative values placed on work and home. Discrimination may not be at work at all.

The impossibility of making such judgments is the fatal flaw of comparable worth. It is a policy that focuses solely on earnings differences between the sexes, without knowing why those differences arose. It is a policy that involves the government, using largely arbitrary techniques, in the minutiae of the wage setting process. It is a heavyhanded approach to a problem that almost everyone admits is extremely subtle. In short, there is no valid reason to adopt comparable worth and plenty of reason not to.

Notes

1. Ronnie J. Steinberg, "Evaluating Jobs," *Society* 22, no. 5, July/August 1985, p. 44.

2. Robert E. Williams, "Comparable Worth: Legal Perspectives and Precedents," *Comparable Worth: Issue for the 80's* (Washington, D.C.: United States Commission on Civil Rights, 1984), pp. 148-149.

3. Earlier figures (1955-1960) come from U.S. Department of Labor, Bureau of Labor Statistics Bulletin 2080, *Perspectives on Working Women: A Data Book* (Washington, D.C.: U.S. Department of Labor, October 1980). Later figures (1960-1982) come from U.S. Department of Labor, Bureau of Labor Statistics Report 710, *Working Women and Public Policy* (Washington, D.C.: U.S. Department of Labor, 1984). These figures will be discussed in more detail below.

4. Reliable estimates of the extensiveness of job evaluation in the private sector are difficult to come by. For several estimates, see Steinberg, "Identifying Wage Discrimination & Implementing Pay Equity Adjustments," p. 101; Donald P. Schwab, "Using Job Evaluation to Obtain Pay Equity," p. 90; and Alvin O. Bellak, "Comparable Worth: A Practitioner's View," p. 82—all in *Comparable Worth: Issue for the 80's.*

5. Herbert R. Northrup, "Comparable Worth and Realistic Wage Setting," *Comparable Worth: Issue for the 80's,* pp. 94-95.

6. Donald J. Treiman and Heidi I. Hartmann, eds., *Women, Work, and Wages: Equal Pay for Jobs of Equal Value* (Washington, D.C.: National Academy Press, 1981), pp. 57-59.

7. *County of Washington v. Gunther,* (452 U.S. 161).

8. Ibid., p. 166.

9. Williams, op. cit., pp. 154-158.

10. [578 F.Supp. 846 (D. Wash. 1983)] See also, Williams, op. cit., pp. 159-161.

11. *Women's Wear Daily,* Wednesday, September 11, 1985, p. 16.

12. Nina Rothchild, "Overview of Pay Initiatives, 1974-1984," *Comparable Worth: Issue for the 80's,* p. 119-128.

13. *HR 3008,* 99th Cong., 1st sess., July 29, 1985. S 519, 99th Cong., 1st sess., February 27, 1985.

14. According to *Billcast* (George Mason University, July 1985), a private computer algorithm which forecasts the likelihood of bills passing, HR 3008 has a 79 percent chance of passing on the floor of the House and S 519 has an 18 percent chance of passing on the floor of the Senate.

15. *HR 375,* 99th Cong., 1st sess., January 3, 1985.

16. *S 5,* 99th Cong., 1st sess., January 3, 1985.

17. Ibid., p. 4.

18. Betty Friedan, *The Feminine Mystique* (New York: Dell Publishing Co., Inc., 1974).

19. Ronald G. Ehrenberg and Robert S. Smith, *Modern Labor Economics: Theory & Public Policy* (Glenview, Illinois: Scott, Foresman & Co., 1982), pp. 329-333.

20. According to the Bureau of Labor Statistics, quoted in the *Wall Street Journal,* June 13, 1985.

21. James P. Smith and Finis Welch, "Affirmative Action and Labor Markets," *Journal of Labor Economics* 2, no. 2, April 1984, pp. 269-298.

22. See Supra, notes 13, 15, and 16.

23. Manhattan Institute for Policy Research, *Manhattan Report on Economic Policy* (New York: Manhattan Institute, 1984), p. 16.

24. "The Wages of Women's Work," *Society* 22, no. 5, July/August 1985, p. 34.

25. Donald J. Treiman and Heidi I. Hartmann, eds., *Women, Work, and Wages* (Washington, D.C.: National Academy Press, 1981), p. 90.

26. See, for example, Joy Ann Grune, "Pay Equity Is a Necessary Remedy for Wage Discrimination, *Comparable Worth: Issue for the 80's,* pp. 166-169; and Andrea H. Beller, "Occupational Segregation and the Earnings Gap," *Comparable Worth: Issue for the 80's,* pp. 31-32.

27. See, for example, Newman and Owen, "Race- and Sex-Based Wage Discrimination is Illegal," *Comparable Worth: Issue for the 80's,* pp. 131-47.

28. Quoted in *Women's Wear Daily,* Sept. 11, 1985, p. 16.

29. American Legislative Exchange Council, *First Reading* 11, no. 9, November 1985, p. 5.

30. Herbert E. Northrup, "Comparable Worth and Realistic Wage Setting," *Comparable Worth: Issue for the 80's,* p. 94.

31. This discussion draws heavily on Schwab, "Using Job Evaluation to Obtain Pay Equity," *Comparable Worth: Issue for the 80's,* pp. 86-88.

32. Bellak, "Comparable Worth: A Practitioner's View," *Comparable Worth: Issue for the 80's,* pp. 79-80.

33. Steinberg, "Identifying Wage Discrimination and Implementing Pay Equity Adjustments," *Comparable Worth: Issue for the 80's,* pp. 99-116.

34. Ibid., p. 104.

35. Ibid., p. 109. Labor economists often refer to this type of study as a hedonic prices study. It is well-known in that literature that the results are sensitive to specification. This is particularly true when the study focuses on many traits which are highly correlated with each other, and when there are many traits relative to the number of observations available. (See Jennifer Roback, "Wages, Rents & the Quality of Life," *Journal of Political Economy* 90, no. 6, 1982, p. 1268.) Both of these conditions are likely to be met in comparable worth studies of individual employers.

36. In New Mexico, for example, a task force was established consisting of eight experienced personnel classification specialists. Each task force member was asked to develop an independent ranking of all state's job classifications—using at least the following factors: skill, effort, responsibility, and working conditions. Half of the raters (four of the eight) could agree on the value of only 8 percent of the jobs analyzed. In other words, four or more raters agreed on the same level for a given job in only 72 of the 896 classifications evaluated. (State of Indiana, "Compensation Task Force Final Report," January 1985, pp. 89-90.)

37. Schwab, op. cit., pp. 89-90.

38. See Supra, note 3.

39. Brigitte Bergen, "At Odds with American Reality," *Society* 22, no. 5, July/August 1985, p. 76.

40. *New York Times,* September 19, 1985.

41. It is interesting to compare the 59 cents figure, which refers to annual earnings to the corresponding figures for weekly earnings.

The ratio of Median Usual weekly earnings of women to men; full time wage and salary workers, 1970-1983.

Date	Female to Male Ratio
1970	62.3
1971	61.7
1972	63.1
1973	61.7
1974	60.8
1975	62.0
1976	62.2
1977	61.9
1978	61.3
1979	62.4
1980	63.4
1981	64.6
1982	65.0
1983	65.6

The ratio of weekly earnings is always greater than 59 percent and this ratio has risen more steadily in the eighties than the ratio of annual earnings. (Earl F. Mellor, "Investigating the Differences in the Weekly Earnings of Women and Men," *Monthly Labor Review* 107, no. 6, June 1984, p. 26, Table 5.)

42. U.S. Department of Commerce, *Statistical Abstract 1984*, p. 413, Table 683.

43. Finis Welch, "Effects of Cohort Size on Earnings: The Baby Boom Babies' Financial Bust," *Journal of Political Economy* 87, no. 5, October 1979, pp. S65-S98.

44. Alan Howard Taylor, "Labor Substitution and the Male-Female Earnings Gap" (unpublished Ph.D. dissertation, Yale University, 1982).

45. U.S. Department of Commerce, *Statistical Abstract 1984*, p. 417, Table 693.

46. James P. Smith and Michael P. Ward, *Women's Wages and Work in the Twentieth Century* (Santa Monica, California: Rand Corporation, 1984). All of the figures quoted from this study refer to weekly, not annual earnings ratios (see Note 41 above).

47. There is another, slightly more sophisticated method of determing discrimination as well. See Ronald L. Oaxaca, "Male-Female Wage Differentials in Urban Labor Markets," *International Economic Review* 14, October 1973, pp. 693-709. However, this method is also a residual method and so shares most of the defects mentioned in the text.

48. Cotton Mather Lindsay, Law and Economics Center, Emory University, Occasional Paper, 1980, "Equal Pay for Comparable Work: An Economic Analysis of a New Antidiscrimination Doctrine," pp. 2-3. This summarizes some of these studies.

49. See S. Rosen, "Human Capital: A Survey of Empirical Research," R. Ehrenberg, ed., *Research in Labor Economics,* 1, 1977 and the studies cited therein.

50. The studies under discussion in this section rely on Census or other government data which include workers from diverse industries, locations, and so on. When individual companies do wage studies of their own work force, they sometimes have access to more extensive information about some of these personality traits.

51. Solomon William Polachek, "Women in the Economy: Perspectives on Gender Inequality," *Comparable Worth: Issue for the 80's;* and Polachek, "Discontinuous Labor Force Participation and Its Effect on Women's Market Earnings," Cynthia Lloyd, ed., *Sex Discrimination & the Division of Labor* (New York: Columbia University Press, 1975), p. 92. See also, *Current Population Reports,* Series P-60, No. 146, April 1985, for figures for 1983.

52. U.S. Department of Labor, Bureau of Labor Statistics Bulletin 2162, *Job Tenure and Occupational Change 1981,* January 1983.

53. Jacob Mincer and Solomon William Polachek, "Family Investments in Human Capital: Earnings of Women," *Journal of Political Economy* 82, March/April 1974, pp. S76-108; and Polachek, "Differences in Expected Post-School Investment as a Determinant of Market Wage Differentials," *International Economic Review* 16, no. 2, 1975, pp. 451-470.

54. Marshall and Paulin, "The Wages of Women's Work," p. 28.

55. Roback, "Torn Between Family and Career? Give Birth to a Business," *Wall Street Journal,* November 14, 1983.

56. Geoffrey Colvin, "What the Baby Boomers Will Buy Next," *Fortune,* October 15, 1984, p. 33.

57. According to Census figures, only 15 percent of the children of full-time working mothers are cared for in group care centers. Nearly half (47 percent) of the children are cared for in other homes. Over a quarter (28.6 percent) of the children are cared for in their own homes, either by their fathers (10.6 percent), or by other relatives (11.4 percent), or by non-relatives (6.6 percent). (Bureau of Census, *Current Population Reports,* P.23, No. 117, p. 6.)

58. Economists almost universally recognize the minimum wage as an ambivalent piece of legislation. Although the benefits of higher

wages are readily apparent, the hidden costs of increased unemployment are just as real. For a survey of evidence on the minimum wage, see Charles Brown, Curtis Gilroy, and Andrew Kohen, "The Effect of the Minimum Wage on Employment & Unemployment," *Journal of Economic Literature* XX, no. 2, June 1982.

59. Lewis M. Terman and Melita H. Oden, *The Gifted Child Grows Up* (Stanford, California: Stanford University Press, 1959), pp. 282-295.

60. *Wall Street Journal,* January 21, 1985, p. 1. This information was provided to the *Journal* by Stanford University sociology professor Lenore Weitzman. Her book *The Divorce Revolution* has just been published by The Free Press.

61. Ibid.

Appendix

99th Congress
1st Session

S. 5

To require the executive branch to enforce applicable equal employment opportunity laws and directives so as to promote pay equity by eliminating wage-setting
practices which discriminate on the basis of sex, race, ethnicity, age, or disability, and result in discriminatory wage differentials.

IN THE SENATE OF THE UNITED STATES

January 3, 1985

Mr. BYRD (for Mr. CRANSTON) (for himself and Mr. MELCHER) introduced the
following bill; which was read twice and referred to the Committee on Govern-
mental Affairs.

A BILL

To require the executive branch to enforce applicable equal employment opportunity laws and directives so as to promote pay equity by eliminating wage-setting
practices which discriminate on the basis of sex, race, ethnicity, age, or disability, and result in discriminatory wage differentials.

*Be it enacted by the Senate and House of Representatives of the United States of
America in Congress assembled,*
That this Act may be cited as the "Pay Equity Act of 1983".

STATEMENT OF FINDINGS AND PURPOSE

Sec. 2 (a) The Congress Finds that—

(1) the average earnings of full-time female workers are significantly lower than the average earnings of similarly situated male workers;

(2) this average earnings difference arises, in significant part, because wages paid in occupational fields or job classifications held predominantly by female workers are lower than those paid in occupational fields or job classifications held predominantly by male workers, and this differential results, in significant part, from the wage-setting practices based on the sex of the employees, rather than any intrinsic differences in the comparable worth of the job as measured by the education, training, skills, experience, effort, responsibility, or working conditions required for the job;

(3) because of these discriminatory wage differentials resulting from discriminatory wage-setting practices, many female workers are underpaid and undercompensated for their work efforts and thereby denied equal employment opportunities;

(4) these discriminatory wage-setting practices and discriminatory wage differentials result in depressing the wages, devaluing the work, and lowering the living standards of many female workers and contribute to the increasing number of women and children living at or near the poverty level and a consequent increase in their need for various forms of government assistance;

(5) the contributions of female workers are vital to our economy, and the continued existence and tolerance of these discriminatory wage-setting practices and discriminatory wage differentials prevent full utilization of the talents, skills, experience, and potential contributions of female workers and result in the exploitation of those workers;

(6) these discriminatory wage-setting practices and discriminatory wage differentials persist despite applicable State and Federal equal opportunity laws and directives;

(7) the Federal agencies charged with the responsibility for enforcement of Federal equal employment opportunity laws and directives have failed to take action, pursuant to applicable such laws and directives, to seek to eliminate discriminatory wage-setting practices and discriminatory wage differentials; and

(8) objective job-evaluation techniques now exist which are utilized by many public and private employers to determine the comparative value of different jobs through a system which numerically rates the basic features and requirements of a particular job, and additional efforts should be made